Oct 2005

# Western Fences

Photography by David R. Stoecklein

# Dedication

For my good friend Darrell Leavitt...

Darrell is one of the true Mackay cowboys. He is one of the guys who loves horses, cows, and the true life of a rancher. I have been lucky enough to spend the last 20 years working and riding with Darrell—branding cattle, roping steers, riding horses, hunting for mule deer and elk, going on pack trips into the Big Lost and Pioneer Mountains, and fly fishing for rainbows and cutthroat trout. Darrell and his lifelong companion, Alice, are members of our family. Darrell is well loved and respected by all who know him in and around Idaho. I am proud to call him my friend.

**Darrell Leavitt,** Bar Horseshoe Ranch, Mackay, Idaho

# Western Fences

Photography—David R. Stoecklein
Editor—Carrie Lightner
Creative director—David R. Stoecklein
Art direction & design—T-Graphics

Cover Photo - **Steve Aslet fixing fence in an ice storm,** Hall Ranch, Bruneau, Idaho
Back Cover Photo - **Rope gate latch,** Duck Valley, Nevada

All images in this book are available as signed original gallery prints and for stock photography usage. Stoecklein Photography houses an extensive stock library of Western, sports, and lifestyle images. David Stoecklein is also an assignment photographer whose clients include Canon, Kodak, Bayer, Hatteras, Marlboro, Chevrolet, Timberland, Ford, Wrangler, Pontiac, and the Cayman Islands.

Other books by Stoecklein Publishing include *The American Quarter Horse, Dude Ranches of the American West, Saddles of the West, The Cowboy Boot, The Spur, The Western Buckle, Ranch Style, The Cowboy Boot, Cowgirls in Heaven, The Performance Horse, Cow Dogs, Lil' Buckaroos, The American Paint Horse, The Idaho Cowboy, Cowboy Gear, Don't Fence Me In, The Texas Cowboys, The Montana Cowboy, The Western Horse, Cowgirls, Spirit of the West,* and *The California Cowboy.*

Every year, Stoecklein Publishing also produces a line of wall calendars, prints, and cards featuring the Western photography of David R. Stoecklein. For more information or to request a catalog, please contact:

Stoecklein Publishing & Photography
Tenth Street Center, Suite A1
Post Office Box 856 • Ketchum, Idaho 83340
tel 208.726.5191  fax 208.726.9752  toll-free 800.727.5191
www.drsphoto.net

Printed in China
Copyright ©2005 by David R. Stoecklein & Stoecklein Publishing

ISBN 1-933192-01-1
Library of Congress Catalog number 2005901825

1 2 3 4 5 6 7 8 9 10 - 09 08 07 06 05

**Opening the gate,** Becky Prunty, Prunty Ranch, Mountain City, Nevada

**Walton Ranch,**
Jackson, Wyoming

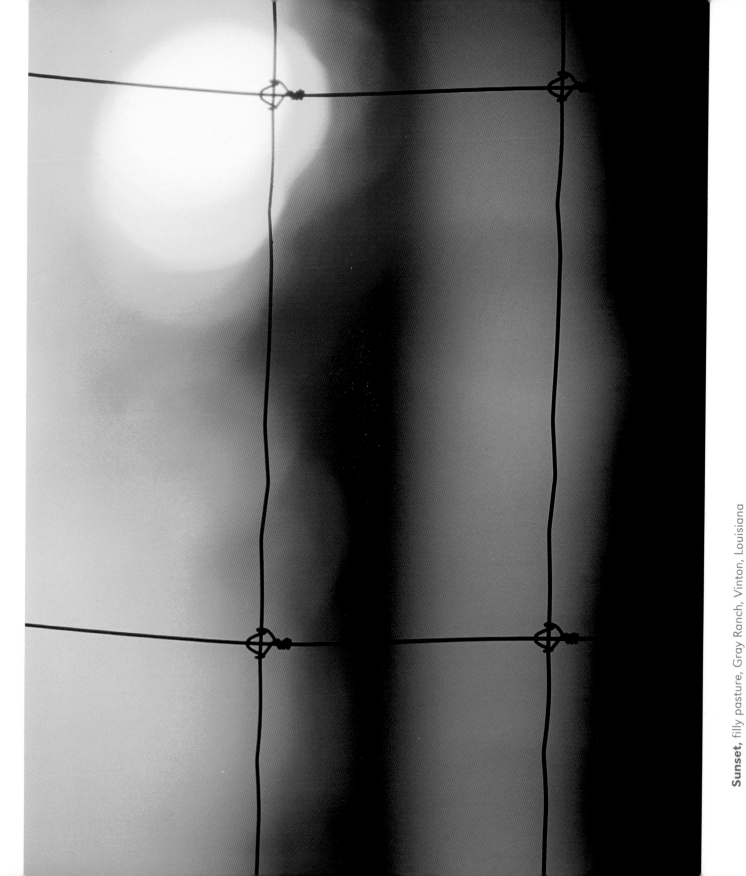

**Sunset,** filly pasture, Gray Ranch, Vinton, Louisiana

8

**The first photo** assignment I ever did was of fences and gates. I took a photography class in college and that is where it all started. I have been doing it now for 36 years and I still always look for great photos of fences wherever my travels take me around the world. The phrase "don't fence me in," means not only that cowboys and cattle and horses shouldn't be fenced in, but also that someone's spirit and freedom should not be fenced in. It is as American as apple pie.

Fences are not only part of my overall passion for taking photographs, they are also a very important part of the West. Therefore they are a big part of my quest to preserve the West by documenting it on film and presenting that vision to my readers through my books, calendars, and prints. Western style, culture, and heritage include the fencing of the West. First, people used barbed wire, or "devil's wire," the wire that ended the era of the open range and was the beginning of the end of the old West and the start of the new West. Before barbed wire, the trail drivers started on the Texas-Mexico border at Brownsville and rode all the way to the Montana-Canada border and never saw a fence or crossed another man's land. The use of barbed wire was originally aimed at controlling cattle for breeding and to keep the bulls separated from the cows. Then it grew into a method for keeping your own cattle in and the neighbor's cattle out. Soon after that, it became a way to claim land and stake out your own piece of the West.

After using barbed wire, Western ranchers started fencing with wooden rails and wooden posts, steel posts and even concrete and granite stone posts. They used boards, rails, pipes, barbed wire, smooth wire, and electric wire in all sorts of different combinations. Geography dictated quite a bit as to what materials were used in different areas of the country. In states where there were large forests of lodgepole pine trees, like Montana, Idaho, and Wyoming, ranchers built fences with log poles and made long jack fences. In the Northwest where big trees were available, men used planks and wide boards to build their fences. In the desert Southwest where nothing much was available at all for fence materials, small sticks and stone corners and braces were used along with steel fence posts.

There were periods of time in U.S. history when the big drift fences were built. Hundreds of thousands of miles of fence went up during the Depression and after World War II. Great fences were built in west Texas and Oklahoma as well as fences to divide the BLM land from Forest Service land in the Northwest. Prisoners in Montana built the great jack fences in the Big Hole and Horse Prairie Valleys.

It is amazing to think about the gangs of men who set out day after day to dig holes, pound posts, and stretch wire up and down the mountainsides in Idaho, Montana, Wyoming, and Oregon in the cold, wet, and heat with only an iron shovel and pliers on a pack horse or in a saddle bag. They cut rails and posts with handsaws and axes, lifting heavy stones and carrying rolls of wire and bundles of iron posts and heavy wooden tubs full of nails and staples. All of this must

Introduction

**Rain hangs on a Powder River gate**, Three Creeks Ranch,
Elk Creek, California

have seemed to be an endless task to them—a fencing job that never ends. Today their work is still holding up well and those fences stand as monuments to their hard work and tenacity.

As the great ranches are split up and reorganized, they are fenced with new materials and built by men with shiny new power tools, tractors, chainsaws, and jeeps. The fences are still straight and still keep the cattle in or out. The fences claim boundaries and set perimeters.

Fences represent culture, design, and function in the true West. There is a lot of pride that goes into building a fence. There are specific fences for horses, cows, sheep, and goats as well as fences for certain types of wildlife or even just for aesthetics. There are certain types of fences for corrals, holding pens, roadways, and trails. You can tell a lot about the owner of a ranch by the way his fences look. You can tell if he raises horses or cows or both. You can also tell how much pride he takes in his land, his business, and his home.

Fencing has to be planned out meticulously; it is essential to think about the kind of materials to use and how much to use and whether to build a five-wire fence or a four-wire fence and whether to use smooth or barbed wire. The gates and alleyways have to be designed for working cattle and sorting horses. The fences have to be placed so that animals can easily reach water, shade, and food.

This book is not meant to be a how-to manual for building fences, but rather a collection of photographs taken all over the West of all kinds of fences. I have chosen these images to educate and inform my readers and also to showcase the art and beauty of the Western fence. I hope you learn a lot about the fences of the West and that you enjoy the beautiful landscapes and unique structures that are all around us and are a part of the scenery.

I also hope that my old photography teacher sees this book and sees that I am still working on that first assignment, even 36 years later.

Keep the spirit of the West alive,

**Ross Goddard,** Bar 13 Ranch,
Mackay, Idaho

**Division fence,** BLM,
Mackay, Idaho

12

**Forest Service fence,**
Togwotee Pass, Wyoming

**Waiting at the gate,**
Horse Prairie Guest Ranch,
Horse Prairie, Montana

**King Ranch Wire**—there is no barbed wire on King Ranch, only King Ranch wire made especially for the ranch. If you stretched all the wire on the ranch in a straight line, it would go from Brownsville, Texas to Portland, Maine.

16

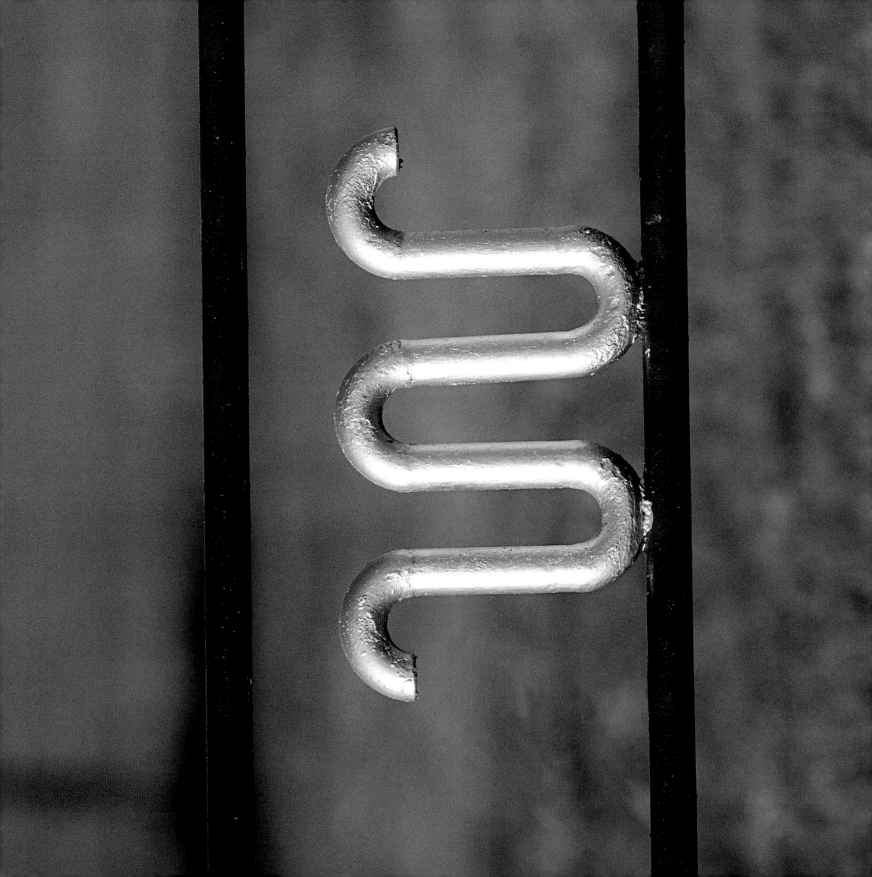

Usually, more than one key or person is needed to enter a gate like this.

**King Ranch gate**, Kingsville, Texas

19

I n the Big Hole Valley of Montana, there is an abundance of lodgepole pine trees. The fences and gates are all made of lodgepole pines—the jacks and the rails. In the winter when the horses are not busy haying, they drag the trees over the snow from the hills to the ranches to be cut for fence building in the summer.

**Dick Hirschy Ranch,**
Big Hole Valley, Montana

**Jack Fence,**
Bar Horseshoe Ranch,
Mackay, Idaho

There is nothing that sets off the landscape like a white board fence. Most of these fences have now been painted black because of the expense of keeping a white fence clean and fresh. There is a lot of pride and hard work that goes into a white fence. A white board or plastic fence makes a powerful statement about the property it protects.

Lazy E Ranch,
Guthrie, Oklahoma

24

**Horseman's gate latch**, Dead Horse Ranch, Chamisal, New Mexico

**Powder River gate latch**

26

# Story of the Devil's Wire

Almost as soon as it started it was over. After the Civil War, the great trail drives started. Great herds of cattle were driven up the trail from Texas to the railheads in Kansas. Cowboys drove the cattle on open prairies that were wild and untamed, just like the cattle, horses, and men on them. Within ten years, the men were driving the cattle to stock the open ranges of Colorado, Wyoming, Montana, and the mines in Idaho. This lasted for only another ten years. By 1880, the ranchers and cattlemen were establishing their ranches and setting up their properties. To do this they needed to keep their cattle in and keep other people's cattle away from their grass and water. Back on the East Coast, the farmers were developing barbed wire to protect their farms and establish boundaries. This new invention of barbed wire, or "devil's wire," eventually made its way to the West and brought a halt to the open range. It cut up the prairie and stopped the cattle drives. It was the end of the era of the freedom of the open range. Devil's wire was the cause of many Western range wars and was also responsible for the West that we know today. Great cattle ranches and empires were formed after barbed wire emerged. The West we know and love was established because of this invention.

Previous page: **Close the gate**, Art Robinson,
Snowline Ranch, Monida, Montana

30

Barbed wire, Nevada

Barbed wire, Texas

**Horse corrals,** Walt Vermedahl Ranch,
Polson, Montana

**Alleyway, sorting corrals,**
Walt Vermedahl Ranch,
Polson, Montana

A stone crib is a box made out of wood or wire that is used to hold a post or to set a corner or a brace when the ground is too wet, muddy, or rocky to hold a fencepost.

**Stone crib,**
Bar Horseshoe Ranch,
Mackay, Idaho

"Good fences make good neighbors."

**Jack Sparrowk and Chet Vogt**, Three Creeks Ranch, Elk Creek, California

This is a log cabin stacked fence that snakes its way along the Sawtooth National Forest in central Idaho. There are over 100 miles of this fence in the valley and it is a beautiful part of the history of the area.

**Veale Ranch,**
Breckenridge, Texas

**Onyx Ranch,** Kern
County, California

**Rupert House Ranch,** East Fork of the Wood River,
Blaine County, Idaho

42

**Red gate,** Prunty Ranch,
Mountain City, Nevada

43

**Board fence,** Lazy E Ranch,
Guthrie, Oklahoma

44

**The corrals at the Eatons' Guest Ranch** in Wolf, Wyoming are some of the most famous in the West. Horses have been wrangled in these corrals for dudes for more than 100 years.

**Haythorn Ranch**, Arthur, Nebraska

On the open ranges of the West, a rope corral is set up to gather the remuda each morning. The cowboys then select their mounts for the day's work. This is a tradition that goes back to the mid-1800s and the great cattle drives.

# Waiting for shipping day

The shipping pens stand frozen and empty under the full moon, waiting to receive cattle in the spring and to ship cattle out in the fall.

**Cornwell Ranch,**
Glasgow, Montana

50

Overhead gates often border a beautiful, natural scene just like a picture frame would. It is not by accident that this happens.

**Overhead gate,** Moosehead Guest Ranch, Grand Teton National Park, Wyoming

**Gate latch,** J.D. Hudgins Ranch,
Hungerford, Texas

**Brahman cattle** stand in a pen looking through
rusted netting, J.D. Hudgins Ranch, Hungerford, Texas

54

**Tall, strong, and true—** gatepost, Diamond A Ranch, Seligman, Arizona

**Barbed wire** embedded in an old oak tree, Three Creeks Ranch, Elk Creek, California

**Diana Wigen fixing fence,** Snowline Ranch, Monida, Montana

# M

**M**ending fences is a great metaphor used throughout our culture. It can refer to everyday life as well as the literal act of fixing a fence that is worn out or broken. People repair fences and relationships. They set boundaries and establish ownership. Fences tie things together and also keep them apart. It is important to keep fences strong and tight, just as it is important to do the same in relationships.

**Skulls**, Beggs Ranch,
Post, Texas

**Skull,** LX Ranch,
Amarillo, Texas

61

**Shipping corrals,** Belmont Park Ranch, Twin Bridges, Montana

**Rope gate latch,** Duck Valley, Nevada

The Parker Ranch is one of the largest ranches in the United States, founded in 1847. This fence stands as a ghost from a time when great sailing merchant ships and whaling vessels visited the island.

**Old stone fence,** Parker Ranch, Big Island, Hawaii

**Wagon wheel fence,** White Stallion
Guest Ranch, Tucson, Arizona

66

**Sunrise,** Big Hole
Valley, Montana

68

**Sunset,** Parker Ranch,
Big Island, Hawaii

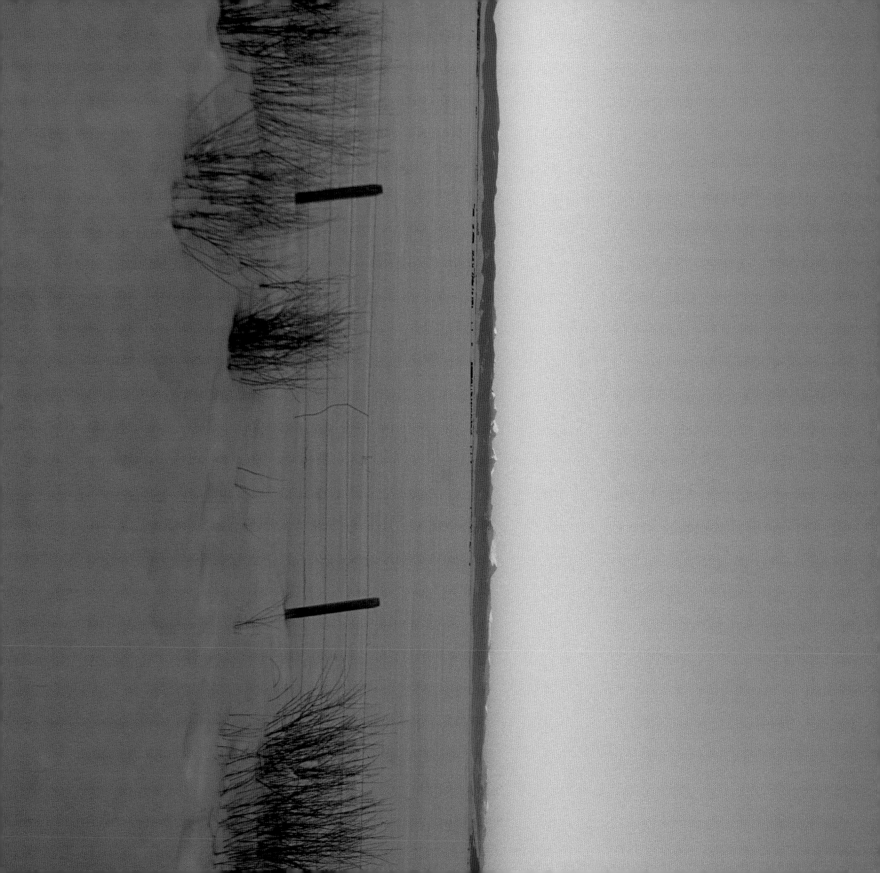

**A peek through the fence** catches a glance of Monique Hack cooling off on a summer day, Mackay, Idaho

**Line camp,** Pitchfork Ranch, Guthrie, Texas

70

71

**Barbed wire,** Three Creeks Ranch,
Elk Creek, California

**Chet Vogt,** Three Creeks Ranch,
Elk Creek, California

72

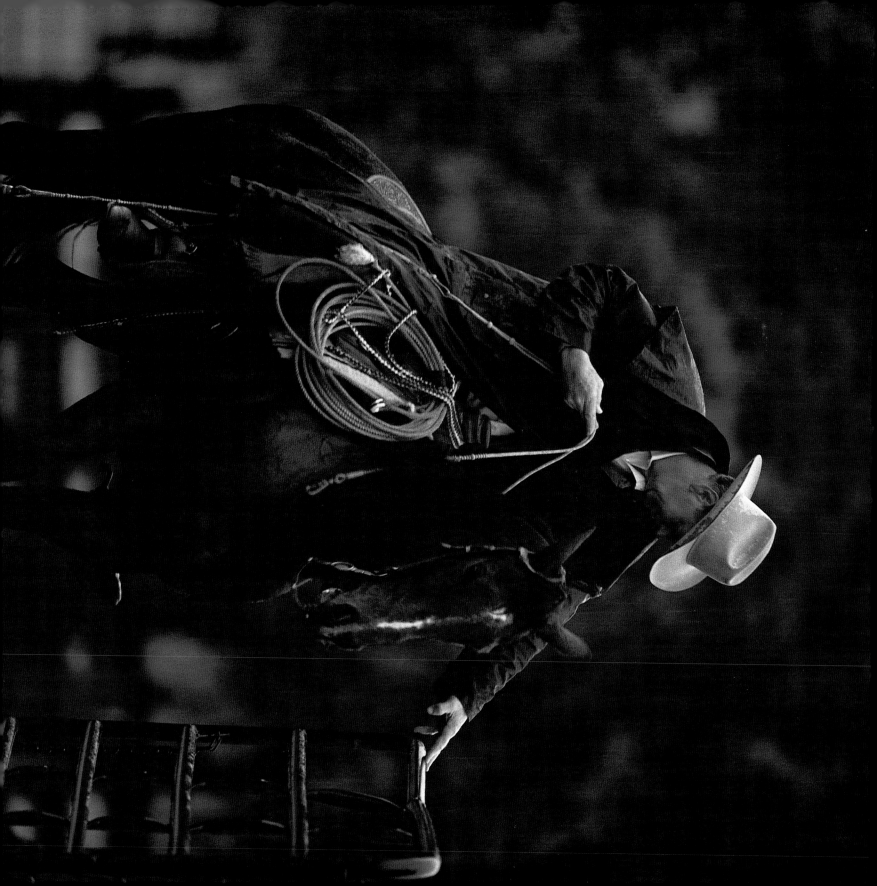

**Gate ornament,** Old Bar 13 Ranch, Mackay, Idaho

74

**Branded fence,** oldest registered brand in
Montana, Matador Ranch, Dillon, Montana

76

# T

here once was a time when coyote hunters across the West hung their trophies from ranch fences. The coyote is still a pest and a problem for livestock owners. However, everyone seems to be living side by side a little better and trophy fences are rarely seen anymore.

**Barton Ranch,**
Carey, Idaho

**Door in adobe wall,** Rancho el Fortin, San Buena Ventura, Mexico

**Adobe walls** guard the Rancho el Fortin, San Buena Ventura, Mexico

78

The saying goes that if you find a gate is closed, leave it closed. If it is open, leave it open. You don't want to let the live-stock out and you sure don't want to keep them from getting water, either.

**Rawhide rope gate**, Binion Ranch, Jordan, Montana

**Entrance gate,** Elkhorn Guest Ranch,
Gallatin Gateway, Montana

**Bill Flournoy** in the shipping
corrals, Likely Land & Livestock,
Likely, California

82

**Curt Pate** sits on the fence and talks to his children, Rial and Mesa, Pate Ranch, Helena, Montana

Manufactured panels, such as these Priefert panels, are being used more and more as moveable fences and as permanent ranch arenas and corrals.

84

**Where great friends meet—**
sitting on the fence, Miller Land
& Livestock, Big Piney, Wyoming

**Frozen wire,**
Medicine Lodge, Idaho

First frost, Picabo, Idaho

87

"Never swing on a gate! It is going to sag, so don't speed it up." -Martin Black to David Stoecklein in 1988, Winecup Ranch, Nevada

**Cowboys of the Dragging Y Ranch,**
Dillon, Montana

89

**J.J.** Gibson was the legendary foreman of the 6666 Ranch. His grave now lies on a hill overlooking the ranch. He loved so much and was loved by many. This small cemetery is the final resting place for many well-loved and respected West Texas cowboys. Casey Daniel's grave lies close to the fence where the cattle pass into the next pasture. It is the same gate he opened many times while he was alive.

**Casey Daniel's gravestone,**
6666 Ranch, Guthrie, Texas

**J.J. Gibson** lies at rest in the 6666 Ranch cemetery, Guthrie, Texas

**Heidi Temmerman,** Bar Horseshoe
Ranch, Mackay, Idaho

**Shadow of a horseman,**
Curt Pate, Helena, Montana

**Innovative gate latch** locks itself when the gate swings
shut, Prunty Ranch, Mountain City, Nevada

94

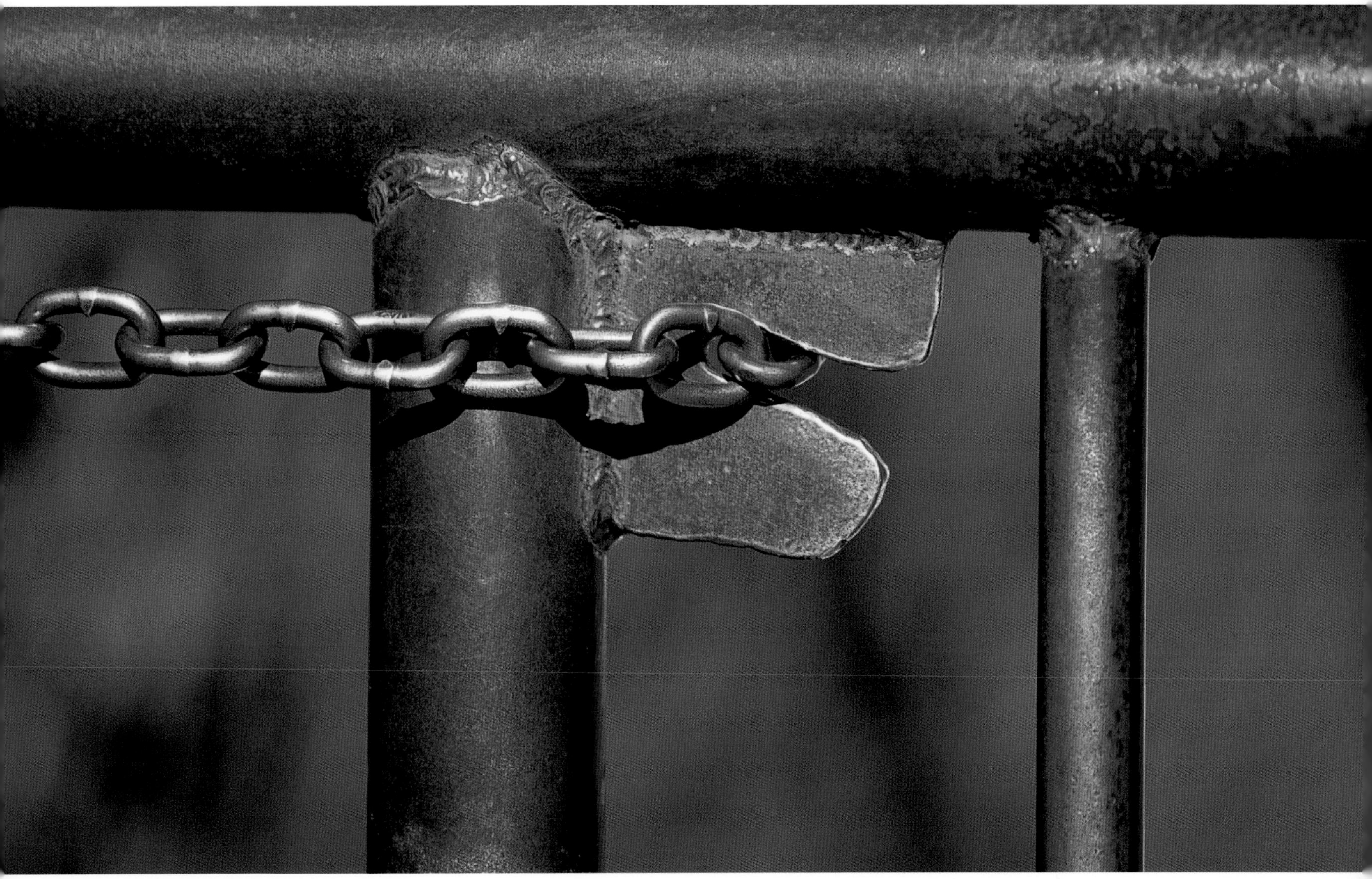

**Ranch-made gate latch,**
Diamond A Ranch,
Seligman, Arizona

A fence is a good place to meet and talk over life. It is often a place to get together and discuss business, family, friendships, and problems that need solving.

**Rob Brown and Jody Bellah,** morning at the RA
Brown Ranch feedlot, Throckmorton, Texas

"Oh, give me land, lots of land under starry skies above, don't fence me in. Let me ride through the wide open country that I love, don't fence me in."

-Cole Porter

**Bar Horseshoe Ranch,**
Mackay, Idaho

**Brandi Coulthard,**
Sun City, Arizona

100

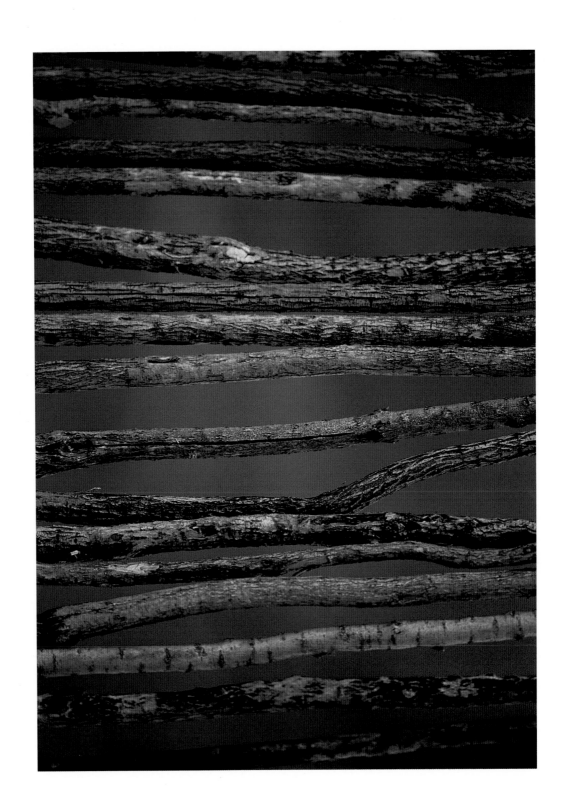

**In the Arizona desert** where there is not much except cactus, sticks are wired together for cattle and horse pens.

**Frozen fence,**
C.A. Ranch, Montana

102

**Iron gate,** Three Creeks Ranch,
Elk Creek, California

# The Laidlaw Fence

A 4,000-acre meadow lies at the heart of Flat Top Sheep Company Ranch in South Central Idaho. This abundant grazing land is surrounded by rolling sagebrush and grass-covered hillsides and basalt rock ridges. But its immediate borders are defined by an imposing fence built by the original ranch owner, Jim Laidlaw, in 1920. It was an extraordinary undertaking at the time to build such a fence and it remains so today.

Laidlaw was a Scotsman and a pioneer in the sheep business, developing the Panama breed of white-faced ewes and introducing the black-faced Suffolk bucks into Idaho. He was not about to watch his prized animals fall prey to marauding coyotes, so he designed and built an enclosure to protect the sheep.

The most notable feature of the fence is its massive Douglas fir corner posts, each one to three feet in diameter. The ends were lightly burned to form a charcoal seal to protect them from rotting. Then the huge corner posts were sunk deeply into the earth with Jim Laidlaw coaching "dig'er a little deeper, boys."

What is less obvious about the structure are the fourteen strands of wire strung between these posts. There are four barbed wires, two planted underground to keep the coyotes from digging beneath the fence, and two strung along the top. These fortify the ten spring-steel wires running horizontally between. Wooden posts and metal stays at regular intervals hold these in place.

The sixteen-mile fence cost $1000 per mile to build, which was an enormous amount at that time. And three-quarters of a century later, it needs only a little repair, only an occasional staple.

Neighbors still admire the fence's workmanship and strength. And they still comment on the scope of the project, amusing themselves with the idea that, in the end, Jim Laidlaw probably fenced in about as many coyotes as he fenced out.

-John and Diane Peavey

**Laidlaw fence,** Flat Top Sheep Company, Carey, Idaho

**Moss-covered board fence,** Fields Livestock, Pleasanton, California

**Log cabin fence,** CM Guest Ranch, Dubois, Wyoming

**Simple wire gate latch,** Hubing Ranch,
Miles City, Montana

**Ranch-made gate latch,**
Hubing Ranch, Miles City, Montana

110

Previous page: **Waiting for dad,** RA Brown Ranch,
Throckmorton, Texas

**Bumper gate,** King Ranch,
Kingsville, Texas

# King Ranch Bumper Gate

These gates were designed so that a cowboy did not have to get out of his truck to open the gate. Instead, he could simply drive slowly through the gate by pushing with the bumper of his truck and the gate would open and then swing shut behind him. A little bit of driving skill is required, of course.

**Ranch-made horseshoe gate latch,**
Bar Horseshoe Ranch, Mackay, Idaho

**5 Dot Ranch,** Susanville, California

**Hirschy Ranch,** Big Hole Valley, Montana

**Bringing in the saddle horses,**
Bar Horseshoe Ranch, Mackay, Idaho

I once asked a cow-boy who was out for the second time that day at 40 degrees below zero why he couldn't take a day like that off. He looked at me like I was crazy and simply replied that the cattle had to eat. There is no such thing as "time off" when your job is to care for livestock. There is no compromise.    —DRS

**Steve Aslet fixing fence**
in an ice storm,
Hall Ranch,
Bruneau, Idaho

118

# Pipe Fence

The oil industry uses tens of thousands of miles of pipe when drilling oil wells all over the West. This salvage pipe is perfect for fences and corrals. The historic fences that were built by the early ranchers are being slowly replaced by these steel pipe versions. The spirit of the West is changing with the progression of time.

**Pipe fence corral,**
Saunders Twin V Ranch,
Weatherford, Texas

**Dude ranch horses** arriving at the corrals,
Nine Quarter Circle Guest Ranch,
Gallatin Gateway, Montana

122

A cow will not jump over this type of gate placed flat on the road. However, a horse will. A cow will not even jump over a cattle guard gate painted on the road. It is somewhat of a mystery as to why this is so, as a cow can jump over a fence easily enough.

**"Texas Gate"** or cattle guard,
Mackay, Idaho

**Winter storm,** Powers Ranch, Leadore, Idaho

**Beaver slide and hay stack,** Powers Ranch, Leadore, Idaho

**Grand gate,** YO Ranch, Mountain Home, Texas

128

**Yard gate,** Dead Horse Ranch, Chamisal, New Mexico

130

**Pasture gate,** Flat Top Sheep Company, Carey, Idaho

131

I n the Sand Hills of Nebraska there is no wood to build permanent branding pens. Panels are carried on a trailer and set up as a temporary pen. Every day during branding season, these pens are set up and then torn down and moved for the next day's work.

**Branding,** Haythorn Land & Cattle Company, Arthur, Nebraska

Once it starts, there is no stopping it. When someone places the first hat or boot on a fencepost, everyone starts doing it and it gets out of control. No one seems to know who is doing it or when, it just happens.

**Barton Flats,** Mackay, Idaho

134

**A great place for horseshoes,**
Bar Horseshoe Ranch, Mackay, Idaho

**Lazy E Ranch,** Guthrie, Oklahoma

**Shipping corrals,** Circle A Ranch,
Mackay, Idaho

**Ranch-made gate—**
the wheel stops the sag,
Binion Ranch, Jordan,
Montana

**Panel latch,** Hubing Ranch, Miles City, Montana

**Rail fence,** 5 Dot Ranch, Susanville, California

**Overhead gate,** 5 Dot Ranch, Susanville, California

Т he overhead on a gate has a function. It holds the fence together. It is a brace. It marks the official entrance to the ranch. Ranchers put everything from expensive ornaments to cow skulls on them.

**Orin Mixer gate,**
Winward Stud Farm,
Purcell, Oklahoma

143

**A cutting horse man lives here,**
Winward Stud Farm, Purcell, Oklahoma

144

A **proud notice that
real cowboys work here,**
Waggoner Ranch, Vernon, Texas

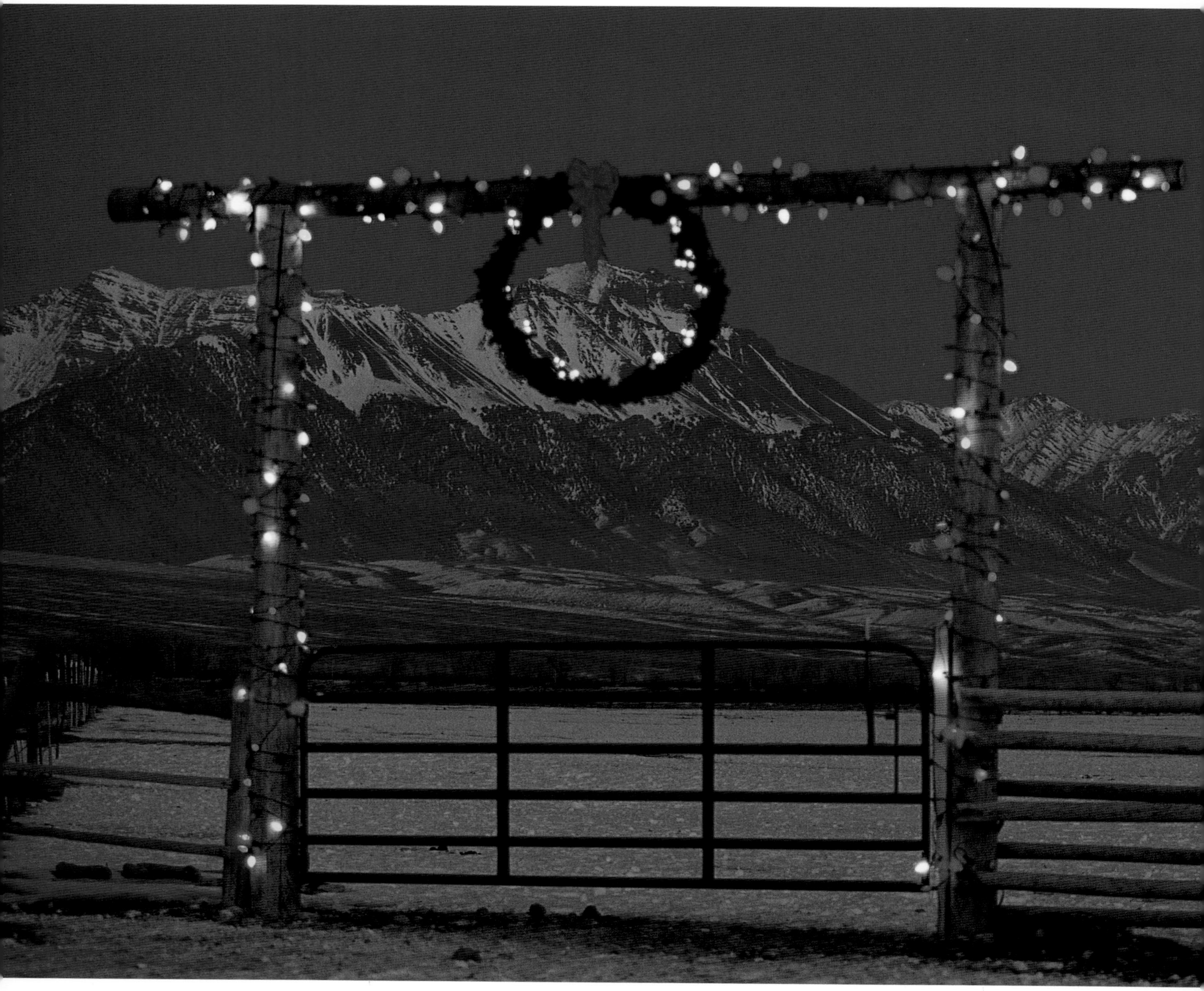

**Jay Hoggan feeding the horses,**
Bar Horseshoe Ranch, Mackay, Idaho

**Christmas gate,**
Bar Horseshoe Ranch,
Mackay, Idaho

147

Y ou can tell who the real cowboy is by where he sits in his pickup truck. He typically drives or sits in the middle. He never sits where he has to get out and open a gate. It also offers a better view for watching a girlfriend or wife struggle with the latch.

**Joni Boyle,**
Menan, Idaho

149

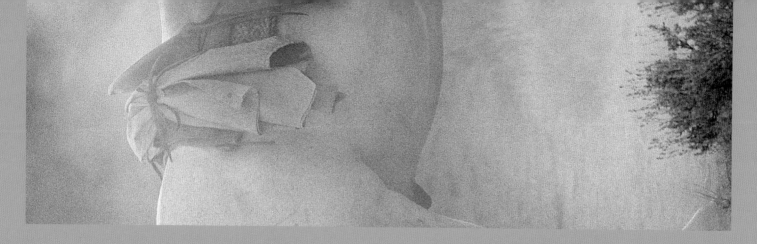

"Don't ever take a fence down until you know why it was put up."

-Robert Frost

Charlie Smith fixing fence in a dust storm, Mackay, Idaho

**Jack fence,**
T Cross Guest Ranch,
Dubois, Wyoming

**Cement post fence,** Rancho el Fortin, San Buena Ventura, Mexico

154

**Cement post,** J.D. Hudgins Ranch,
Hungerford, Texas

**Sunset over
jack fence,**
Sheridan Ranch,
Mackay, Idaho

156

Sitting on the fence can mean a lot of things—indecision, waiting out the competition, taking a break, watching the action, or just plain sitting on the fence and enjoying life.

**Becky Prunty,**
Prunty Ranch,
Mountain City,
Nevada

159

In the morning before the sun comes up, the cowboys gather at the corrals. They select their horse for the day's work, receive their morning orders, and head out the gate. The corral is a gathering place, like homeroom in high school. It is where the day starts and ends.

**Veale Ranch,**
Breckenridge, Texas

# The Stoecklein Mission

David Stoecklein has spent a lifetime documenting the West on film. His personal and professional quest in life is to preserve the West. This small volume is an important part of that quest to save, honor, and educate.

Keep the spirit of the West alive!

**Dave Stoecklein at work on his ranch,**
Bar Horseshoe Ranch, Mackay, Idaho

# Other Books from Stoecklein Publishing

The American Quarter Horse
Dude Ranches of the American West
Saddles of the West
The Cowboy Boot
The Western Buckle
The Spur
Cowgirls in Heaven
Ranch Style
The Performance Horse
Lil' Buckaroos
Cow Dogs
Spirit of the West

The American Paint Horse
The California Cowboy
The Idaho Cowboy
Cowboy Gear
The Montana Cowboy
Don't Fence Me In
Cowgirls
The Texas Cowboys
The Western Horse
Sun Valley Images
Sun Valley Signatures I, II, III

# Technical Notes

I use Kodak film and Canon cameras and lenses for all the photography in my books and in my commercial work as well. I use a variety of different cameras from Canon, mostly the EOS 1N and the 1V. As for lenses, I use the 300mm and 400mm f/2.8L IS USM and the 16-35mm and 28-70mm f/2.8L USM and 70-200mm f/2.8L IS USM zooms. I also use prime lenses like the 20mm f/2.8 USM, 35mm and 50mm f/1.4 USM. I use the Canon Image Stabilizer lens whenever I can, which happens to be most of the time.

All of the slide film for this project was processed at the BWC Photo Imaging lab in Dallas, Texas. They have been processing the film for all of my books as well as the 35mm film for my regular assignments for the last thirteen years. We have a great working relationship, one that is essential in this line of work to maintain consistency and accuracy. All of the scans for this book were done at T-graphics/Express Printing in Hailey, Idaho.

I am extremely lucky to have all the good people at Canon USA and BWC as well as the staff in my Ketchum studio as a support team while I fly around the country on assignments. Without all of them, my job would be much more difficult.

-DRS

# Thank You

I hope that you enjoyed this book of fence photographs as much as I enjoyed taking them and organizing them into this small book. I hope this book gives you, the reader, a greater understanding and appreciation for the West that we all know and love today. Thank you to all my friends and fans.

-DRS

166